YOU'RE THE CHEF

TERRIFIC Veggies ON THE SIDE

Kari Cornell Photographs by **Brie Cohen**

M MILLBROOK PRESS • MINNEAPOLIS

For my mom, who taught me how to experiment in the kitchen; and for Will, Theo, and Brian, who cheerfully sampled every veggie I put on the table —K.C.

For Joe Stafford. Thank you for your time and wisdom. —B.C.

Photography by Brie Cohen
Food in photographs prepared by chef David Vlach
Illustrations by Laura Westlund/Independent Picture Service
The image on page 5 is used with the permission of © iStockphoto.com/stuartbur.

Allergy alert: The recipes in this book contain ingredients to which some people can be allergic. Anyone with food allergies or sensitivities should follow the advice of a physician or other medical professional.

Millbrook Press
A division of Lerner Publishing Group, Inc.
241 First Avenue North
Minneapolis, MN 55401 U.S.A.

Website address: www.lernerbooks.com

Main body text set in Felbridge Std Regular 11/14.
Typeface provided by Monotype Typography.

Library of Congress Cataloging-in-Publication Data

Cornell, Kari A.
Terrific veggies on the side /
by Kari Cornell ; photographs by Brie Cohen.
pages cm. — (You're the chef)
Includes index.
ISBN 978–0–7613–6640–9 (lib. bdg. : alk. paper)
ISBN 978–1–4677–1716–8 (eBook)
1. Cooking (Vegetables) 2. Side dishes (Cooking)
I. Cohen, Brie, illustrator. II. Title.
TX801.C6287 2014
641.6'5—dc23   2012048909

Manufactured in the United States of America
1 – CG – 7/15/13

TABLE of CONTENTS

Are you ready to make some terrific veggies on the side? YOU can be the chef and make food for yourself and your family. These easy recipes are perfect for a chef who is just learning to cook. And they're so delicious, you'll want to make them again and again!

I developed these recipes with the help of my kids, who are six and eight years old. They can't do all the cooking on their own yet, but they can do a lot.

Can't get enough of cooking? Check out www.lerneresource.com for bonus recipes, healthful eating tips, links to cooking technique videos, and more!

BEFORE YOU START

Reserve your space! Always ask for permission to work in the kitchen.

Find a helper! You will need an adult helper for some tasks. Talk with this person to decide what steps you can do on your own and what steps the adult will help with.

Make a plan! Read through the whole recipe before you start cooking. Do you have the ingredients you'll need? If you don't know what a certain ingredient is, see page 31 to find out more. Do you understand each step? If you don't understand a technique, such as *sprinkle* or *slice*, turn to page 7. At the beginning of each recipe, you'll see how much time you'll need to prepare the recipe and to cook it. The recipe will also tell you how many servings it makes. Small drawings at the top of each recipe let you know what major kitchen equipment you'll need—such as a stovetop, a blender, or a microwave.

stovetop

blender

knives

microwave

oven

Wash up! Always wash your hands with soap and water before you start cooking. And wash them again after you touch raw eggs, meat, or fish.

Get it together! Find the tools you'll use, such as measuring cups or a mixing bowl. Gather all the ingredients you'll need. That way you won't have to stop to look for things once you start cooking.

SAFETY TIPS

That's sharp! Your adult helper needs to be in the kitchen when you are using a knife, a grater, or a peeler. If you are doing the cutting, use a cutting board. Cut away from your body, and keep your fingers away from the blade.

That's hot! Be sure an adult is in the kitchen if you use the stove or the oven. Your adult helper can help you cook on the stove and take hot things out of the oven.

Tie it back! If you have long hair, tie it back or wear a hat. If you have long sleeves, roll them up. You want to keep your hair and clothing out of the food and away from flames or other heat sources.

Turn that handle! When cooking on the stove, turn the pot handle toward the back. That way, no one will accidentally bump the pot and knock it off the stove.

Wash it! If you are working with raw eggs or meat, you need to keep things extra clean. After cutting raw meat or fish, wash the knife and the cutting board right away. They must be clean before you use them to cut anything else.

Go slowly! Take your time when you're working. When you are doing something for the first time, such as peeling or grating, be sure not to rush.

Above all, have fun!

Finish the job right!

One of your most important jobs as a chef is to clean up when you're done. Wash the dishes with soap and warm water. Wipe off the countertop or the table. Put away any unused ingredients. The adults in your house will be more excited for you to cook next time if you take charge of cleaning up.

COOKING TOOLS

bowls

colander

cookie sheet

cutting board

deep pie pan

dry measuring cups

fork

frying pan

grater

knives

liquid measuring cup

measuring spoons

oven mitt

potato masher

saucepans

scrub brush

serrated knife

spatula

spoon

stockpot

tongs

vegetable peeler

whisk

wooden spoon

TECHNIQUES

boil: to heat liquid on a stovetop until it starts to bubble

chop: to cut food into small pieces using a knife

cover: to put a lid on a pan or pot containing food

discard: to throw away or put in a compost bin. Discarded parts of fruits and vegetables and eggshells can be put in a compost bin, if you have one.

drain: to pour the liquid off a food. You can drain food by pouring it into a colander or strainer. If you are draining water or juice from canned food, you can also use the lid to hold the food back while the liquid pours out.

drizzle: to slowly pour or dribble a thin stream of liquid over food

fry: to cook in a pan, usually in oil or butter, until lightly browned and cooked through

grate: to use a food grater to shred food into small pieces

grill: to cook on a gas or charcoal grill outside

mash: to smash cooked pieces of food into a creamy mixture using a potato masher or electric mixer

mix: to stir food using a spoon or fork

preheat: to turn the oven to the temperature you will need for baking. An oven takes about 15 minutes to heat up.

serrated: a tool, such as a knife, that has a bumpy edge

set aside: to put nearby in a bowl or plate or on a clean workspace

slice: to cut food into thin pieces

sprinkle: to scatter on top

toss: to mix food with a sauce or dressing in a bowl until food pieces are completely coated

whisk: to stir or whip with a whisk or fork

MEASURING

To measure **dry ingredients**, such as sugar or flour, spoon the ingredient into a measuring cup until it is full. Then use the back of a butter knife to level it off. Do not pack it down unless the recipe tells you to. Do not use measuring cups made for liquids.

When you're measuring a **liquid**, such as milk or water, use a clear glass or plastic measuring cup. Set the cup on the table or a counter and pour the liquid into the cup. Pour slowly and stop when the liquid has reached the correct line.

Don't measure your ingredients over the bowl they will go into. If you accidentally spill, you might have way too much!

serves 4 to 6

preparation time: 15 minutes
baking time: 20 minutes

ingredients:

2 large sweet potatoes
⅛ cup olive oil
1 teaspoon salt
¼ teaspoon ground
   black pepper
½ teaspoon sugar
¼ teaspoon chili powder
ketchup or other favorite
   dipping sauce

equipment:

paper towels
vegetable peeler
knife
cutting board
large mixing bowl
liquid measuring cup
tongs
measuring spoons
small plastic container with
   tight-fitting lid
cookie sheet with sides
oven mitts
spatula

Sweet Potato Oven Fries

These tasty fries are a nice stand-in for the salty, fried white potato version. And they're much better for you!

1. **Preheat** the oven to 450°F.

2. **Wash** sweet potatoes in cool water and pat dry.

3. Use a vegetable peeler to **peel** the skin off the sweet potatoes. Discard the skins. Use a knife and a cutting board to **cut** a sweet potato in half lengthwise. Place one of the halves cut side down on the cutting board. Cut the sweet potato lengthwise into ½-inch-wide slices. Then arrange the slices cut side down on the cutting board. Cut each slice lengthwise into ½-inch-wide fries. Repeat with the other half of the sweet potato. Then repeat the entire process for the second sweet potato.

4. **Place** the cut fries in a large mixing bowl. **Add** olive oil. Use tongs to **toss** the potatoes in the oil. Be sure all the slices are well coated.

5. In a small plastic container with a lid, **combine** salt, ground black pepper, sugar, and chili powder. **Cover** tightly with the lid, and **shake** well to mix spices.

6. Spread the fries on a cookie sheet, and **sprinkle** evenly with spice mixture.

7. Use oven mitts to **place** the cookie sheet in the oven. **Bake** for 10 minutes.

8. Use oven mitts to **remove** the cookie sheet from the oven, and place the cookie sheet on top of the stove. Use a spatula to **flip** the fries over. **Place** the cookie sheet back in the oven, and **bake** for another 10 minutes.

9. Use oven mitts to **remove** the cookie sheet from the oven. Allow the fries to cool slightly. Serve with ketchup or your favorite dipping sauce.

TRY THIS!

This recipe is tasty with white potatoes too. Yukon gold potatoes make great fries! Leave out the sugar and chili powder. Instead, sprinkle with 1 tablespoon dried parsley when you remove the potatoes from the oven.

Try using different spices. If you're not a fan of chili powder, try cinnamon or cumin instead. Or just use plain old salt and ground black pepper.

serves 4

preparation time: 20 minutes
cooking time: 18 minutes

ingredients:

2 medium white potatoes,
  any variety
1 medium zucchini
1 medium carrot
1 green onion
2 eggs
¼ cup skim milk
1 teaspoon minced garlic,
  from a jar
¼ teaspoon ground black pepper
1 teaspoon salt
1 tablespoon canola oil
applesauce, sour cream,
  or plain yogurt

equipment:

paper towels
large mixing bowl
whisk
liquid measuring cup
measuring spoons
knife
cutting board
vegetable grater
measuring cups—1 cup, ¼ cup
wooden spoon
large frying pan
spatula
serving plate

Zucchini Potato Pancakes

These crispy treats are easy to make and taste great with a dollop of sour cream, plain yogurt, or applesauce. Make them as a side dish with fish or as the main course with a side salad.

1. **Wash** the potatoes, the zucchini, the carrot, and the green onion in cool water. Pat dry and set aside.

2. **Crack** the eggs into a large mixing bowl. **Add** milk, minced garlic, ground black pepper, and salt to the eggs. **Whisk** until well mixed.

3. Use a grater to **grate** the potatoes—skin and all—over a cutting board. Grate enough to measure 2 cups. **Add** the grated potatoes to the egg mixture.

4. Use the cutting board, the knife, and the grater to prepare the zucchini and the carrots. For the zucchini, **cut** off the ends and discard. **Grate** the zucchini—skin and all—over the cutting board until you have enough to measure ¾ cup. **Add** the grated zucchini to the egg mixture.

5. For the carrots, **cut** off the stem end and the very tip, if damaged. Discard these trimmings. **Grate** the carrot—skin and all—over the cutting board until you have enough to measure ¼ cup. **Add** the grated carrot to the egg mixture.

6. To chop the green onion, **cut** off the roots and discard. Remove any dry or wilted green parts. Then **slice** the onions into thin rounds. You can use both the white and green parts of the onion. **Add** the sliced onion to the egg mixture.

Turn the page for more Zucchini Potato Pancakes

TRY THIS!

Try using different vegetables with the potatoes. Anything that will grate well is fair game. Sweet potatoes, yams, kohlrabi, cabbage, or even finely chopped broccoli are all tasty. Be sure to steam kohlrabi, cabbage, or broccoli for 5 minutes, and allow it to cool before adding to the potatoes. The grated vegetables should measure 3 cups total.

7. Use a wooden spoon to thoroughly **mix** all the grated vegetables with the egg mixture.

8. **Pour** canola oil into a large frying pan. Turn the burner under the frying pan on medium-high. Use a spatula to evenly **spread** the oil around the pan. Allow the pan to warm for 2 minutes. While the pan is warming, **place** a paper towel on a serving plate.

9. Use a ¼-cup measuring cup to **scoop** the batter from the bowl into the frying pan. Repeat 2 to 3 more times, making sure to leave 1 inch between each pancake. (You should be able to cook 4 pancakes at a time, depending on the size of your frying pan.)

10. Cook for about 3 minutes. Then use the spatula to **flip** the pancakes. Cook for about 3 more minutes on the second side. When done, the pancakes should be golden brown on both sides. Use the spatula to move the pancakes to the serving plate with the paper towel.

11. **Repeat** steps 9 and 10 until the batter is gone. If needed, add additional oil to the frying pan for each new batch. Enjoy the potato pancakes warm with a scoop of sour cream, plain yogurt, or applesauce on top.

Easy Refrigerator Pickles

Here's your chance to impress your friends and family with your very own batch of homemade pickles! These sweet-salty treats are quick to make. But they need to chill for a few days for best flavor.

1. **Wash** canning jars or containers and lids in hot, soapy water. Rinse well and allow to air-dry.

2. **Wash** cucumbers in cool water. Scrub the skin with a kitchen brush to remove any dirt. Pat dry.

Turn the page for more Easy Refrigerator Pickles

serves 8 to 10

preparation time: 10 minutes
cooking time: 5 minutes
chilling time: 4 days

ingredients:

2 to 3 large cucumbers
1 small onion
3 garlic cloves
1½ cups rice vinegar
½ cup water
¾ cup sugar
¾ teaspoon salt
½ teaspoon celery salt
½ teaspoon mustard seeds
½ leaspoon red pepper flakes
2 whole cloves

equipment:

3 2-cup canning jars or other 2-cup containers with tight-fitting lids
dish soap
vegetable scrub brush
paper towels
knife
cutting board
measuring cups—½ cup, ¼ cup
medium saucepan
liquid measuring cup
measuring spoons
wooden spoon

Easy Refrigerator Pickles continued

3. Use a knife and a cutting board to cut the cucumbers and the onion. To cut the cucumbers, **cut** off and discard the ends. **Slice** the cucumbers into thin rounds until you have enough to fill 3 cups. Set aside.

4. To cut the onion, **cut** off both ends. Set the onion on one of the flat parts you made by cutting it. Cut the onion in half. **Peel** off and discard the papery layers around the outside. Lay the onion half flat on the cutting board. **Chop** the onion crosswise into thin, semicircular slices. **Pile** slices into a ½-cup measuring cup. Set aside.

5. **Peel** and discard the white, papery skin from the garlic cloves. **Place** one garlic clove in each clean jar or container.

6. **Place** ⅓ of the onion slices and cucumber slices in layers at the bottom of one jar or container. Repeat with the other two jars.

7. In a medium saucepan, **combine** rice vinegar, water, sugar, salt, celery salt, mustard seeds, red pepper flakes, and whole cloves. **Stir** with a wooden spoon until well mixed. Turn the burner under the saucepan on high. Bring the vinegar mixture to a boil.

8. Ask an adult to help you **pour** ⅓ of the vinegar mixture over the layered cucumbers and onions in each jar. If needed, use additional water so that the cucumbers are completely covered.

9. **Place** the lids on all the jars or containers. Allow to cool on the counter for 3 hours.

10. **Place** pickles in the refrigerator for 4 days before eating. Enjoy with sandwiches or all by themselves!

TRY THIS!

If you don't have rice vinegar, use plain vinegar instead.

Add thin slices of small red or yellow peppers to your pickles.

Use zucchini slices instead of cucumber slices.

If small pickling cucumbers are available, you can use 3 to 4 cups of whole cucumbers instead of slices.

Add a sprig of fresh dill to each of the jars.

serves 4 to 6

preparation time: 10 minutes
cooking time: 10 to 15 minutes

ingredients:

6 red or Yukon gold potatoes,
   the size of an adult's fist
2 tablespoons butter
¼ cup half-and-half
¼ cup grated Parmesan cheese
1 teaspoon minced garlic, from
   a jar
1 teaspoon salt
¼ teaspoon ground
   black pepper

equipment:

vegetable scrub brush
paper towels
cutting board
knife
large saucepan
fork
colander
potato masher
measuring spoons
liquid measuring cup
measuring cup—¼ cup
spoon

Creamy Mashed Potatoes

Who doesn't love a scoop or two of creamy, buttery mashed potatoes on a cold winter's day? Roll up your sleeves and get ready to do some mashing!

1. **Wash** the potatoes in cold water, using a scrub brush to remove any dirt. Pat dry.

2. Using a cutting board and a knife, **cut** the unpeeled potatoes into 1-inch circles. Then **chop** each slice into large chunks.

3. **Place** the cut potatoes into a large saucepan. **Add** enough water so the potatoes have 2 inches of water over the top of them.

4. Turn the burner under the pan on high. Bring the potatoes to a boil. **Boil** them for 10 to 15 minutes, or until a fork can be easily inserted into one of the potato pieces. When the potatoes are done cooking, have an adult **drain** them into a colander.

5. **Pour** the drained potatoes back into the saucepan. Use a potato masher to **mash** the potatoes until they are smooth.

6. In the saucepan, **add** butter, half-and-half, grated Parmesan cheese, minced garlic, salt, and ground black pepper. **Mash** and **stir** into the potatoes using the masher.

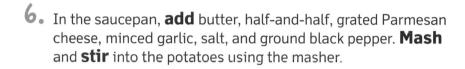

7. **Taste** to check seasoning, and add more salt or ground black pepper if needed. Serve hot!

TRY THIS!

If you don't like the taste of garlic, you can leave it out.

Add 1 cup cleaned, chopped cauliflower florets to the boiling potatoes for the last 7 minutes of cooking time. Then drain and mash the cauliflower with the potatoes.

To lighten this dish, substitute ¼ cup plain, low-fat yogurt for the half-and-half and add only 1 tablespoon butter.

Crispy Kale Chips

If you like potato chips, try this recipe. The kale leaves crisp up nicely. Best of all, kale is really good for you. It's packed with vitamin A, vitamin K, and iron.

serves 4

preparation time: 10 minutes
baking time: 9 minutes

ingredients:
1 bunch fresh kale
1 tablespoons olive oil
1½ teaspoons salt

equipment:
paper towels
measuring spoons
medium bowl
tongs
2 cookie sheets, with sides
oven mitts
spatula
serving bowl

1. **Preheat** the oven to 375°F.

2. **Wash** kale leaves in cool water and pat dry.

3. Use your (clean) hands to **pull** the leafy parts of the kale away from the central stem. Discard the stem. Then **tear** the leaves into bite-size pieces.

4. **Place** the kale pieces in a medium bowl. **Add** oil and salt. Use tongs to **toss** the kale until all the pieces are well coated.

5. **Spread** the kale onto 2 cookie sheets. Use oven mitts to **place** the sheets in the oven. **Bake** for 7 minutes.

6. Use oven mitts to open the oven and **remove** the cookie sheets. **Flip** the kale pieces over with a spatula. Return the sheets to the oven, and **bake** for 2 minutes more. Transfer to a serving bowl and enjoy!

TRY THIS!

For extra flavor, sprinkle kale leaves with ⅛ cup grated **Parmesan** cheese before baking.

serves 4 to 8

preparation time: 1 hour, 15 minutes
baking time: 40 minutes

ingredients:

1 cup wild rice
2 acorn squash
1 apple
4 tablespoons olive oil
½ cup dried apricots
1 small onion
¼ cup chicken or vegetable stock
¼ cup dried cranberries
½ cup pecan pieces
1 teaspoon salt
¼ teaspoon ground black pepper
1 teaspoon thyme
⅓ cup bread crumbs
4 tablespoons butter
4 teaspoons real maple syrup

equipment:

medium saucepan with lid
paper towels
cutting board
knife
spoon
measuring spoons
2 cookie sheets with sides
oven mitts
measuring cups—½ cup, ⅓ cup,
   ¼ cup
medium frying pan
wooden spoon
liquid measuring cup
spatula

Sensational Stuffed Squash

This is a yummy way to make squash in the fall. Serve it as a side dish with roasted turkey or chicken—or make it a main course!

1. In a medium saucepan, **cook** the wild rice according to package directions.

2. **Arrange** two of the oven racks in the center of the oven, making sure there's enough space between them to allow for the squash. **Preheat** the oven to 350°F.

3. **Wash** the squash and the apple under cool water, and pat dry.

4. Have an adult **cut** each squash in half from top to bottom. Use a spoon to **scoop** out and discard the seeds.

5. **Pour** 1 tablespoon olive oil onto each cookie sheet. Use a paper towel to spread the oil evenly around the sheet.

6. **Place** the squash halves, cut side down, on the cookie sheets. Use oven mitts to place the cookie sheets in the center of the oven. **Bake** for 30 minutes.

Turn the page for more
Sensational Stuffed Squash

7. While the squash is baking, use the knife and the cutting board to cut the apple, apricots, and onion. To cut the apple, first, **cut** it in half from top to bottom. Cut one of the halves in half again from top to bottom. Then cut out and discard the stem and the seeds. **Chop** into ¼-inch pieces. Repeat with the other half. Set aside.

8. To cut the dried apricots, **chop** them into small pieces and set aside.

9. To cut the onion, **cut** off both ends. Set the onion on one of the flat parts you made by cutting it. Cut the onion in half. **Peel** off and discard the papery layers around the outside. Lay the onion half flat on the cutting board. Cut the onion crosswise into semicircular slices. Then **chop** the slices into small pieces. Repeat with the other half. Cut enough to measure ½ cup. Set aside.

10. **Pour** 2 tablespoons olive oil in a medium frying pan. Turn the burner under the frying pan on medium. **Add** onions to the pan. **Fry** for 7 minutes, stirring with the wooden spoon. **Add** the chopped apples to the pan, and **fry** for 5 minutes.

11. **Add** chicken or vegetable stock, chopped apricots, dried cranberries, pecan pieces, salt, ground black pepper, thyme, and cooked wild rice to the frying pan. **Stir** with the wooden spoon to combine. **Add** bread crumbs, and stir again. Heat for 5 minutes. Then turn off the burner.

12. Once the squash has baked for 30 minutes, use oven mitts to **remove** the cookie sheets from the oven. Set them on top of the stove. Ask an adult to help you use a spatula to **turn** each hot squash over so that the cut side faces up.

13. Use a ½-cup measuring cup to **scoop** ½ cup of the wild rice mixture into each squash half. Top each stuffed squash with 1 tablespoon butter, and **drizzle** with 1 teaspoon real maple syrup.

14. Use oven mitts to return both cookie sheets to the oven. **Bake** for another 10 minutes. Then use oven mitts to **remove** the cookie sheets from the oven. Serve warm.

TRY THIS!

For a less sweet version, leave out the butter and maple syrup. Instead, top each squash half with 1 tablespoon crumbled **blue cheese** or grated **Parmesan cheese.**

You can substitute other **dried fruits** or **nuts** for the apricots, cranberries, and pecans. **Dried cherries** or **raisins** with **walnuts, hazelnuts, pine nuts,** or chopped **almonds** are also delicious.

Buttery Corn on the Cob

serves 6

preparation time: 15 minutes
cooking time: 7 minutes

ingredients:
6 fresh ears of corn
1 stick butter
salt and ground black pepper
to taste

equipment:
paper grocery bag
large stockpot
butter plate
tongs
serving plate

Corn on the cob is a favorite summertime treat.
For the best-tasting corn, wait until corn is in season
in your part of the country. The fresher the corn,
the better the flavor!

1. Take a paper grocery bag and the ears of corn outside to husk. Simply **peel** back the green leaves and yellow strands of "silk" that cover the cob of corn. Break off the stem, and **discard** all leaves, silk, and stems in the paper bag.

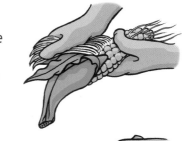

2. Carry the cobs back inside, and **wash** them in cool water.

3. **Place** the cobs in a large stockpot, and **fill** with plenty of water. The water should be 2 inches above the cobs.

4. Turn the burner under the pot on high. Bring the pot of water to a full boil. Then **boil** the corn for 3 minutes.

24

5. As the cobs cook, unwrap the stick of butter and **place** it on a butter plate.

6. When the corn is done, it should be bright yellow. Turn off the burner, and ask an adult to help you use tongs to carefully **place** the hot corncobs on a serving plate.

7. **Serve** with butter, salt, and ground black pepper.

TRY THIS!

Serve with **lemon slices**, and squeeze lemon juice on the hot, buttered cobs.

With an adult's help, you can roast corn on the grill. As the adult gets the grill ready, peel off a few outer leaves, but leave the rest on. Soak cobs in a sink filled with cool water for 1 hour. Place leaf-covered cobs on the grill, and cook covered for about 30 minutes. Have an adult turn the corn every 10 minutes until each side is browned or lightly blackened. Let the cobs cool a bit. Then peel off and discard the leaves and silk.

serves 4 to 6

preparation time: 15 minutes
cooking time: 0 minutes

ingredients:

1 teaspoon minced garlic, from
  a jar
½ cup plain, low-fat yogurt
½ cup sour cream
2 tablespoons mayonnaise
1 teaspoon dill
¼ teaspoon ground black pepper
½ teaspoon salt
1 cup each: baby carrots, cherry
  tomatoes, sugar snap peas,
  radishes
1 large cucumber

equipment:

small mixing bowl
measuring cups—1 cup, ½ cup
measuring spoons
fork
small serving bowl
plastic wrap
paper towels
knife
cutting board
serving plate

Veggies with Homemade Dill Dip

Fresh, crunchy vegetables dipped in a delicious, creamy dip are great for taking the edge off hunger before dinnertime. And they're good for you too!

1. **Add** minced garlic, yogurt, sour cream, mayonnaise, dill, ground black pepper, and salt to a small mixing bowl. **Stir** well with a fork. Transfer to a small serving bowl for dipping. Cover the bowl with plastic wrap, and refrigerate until ready to serve.

2. Use a measuring cup to **measure** carrots, tomatoes, sugar snap peas, and radishes. **Wash** them and the cucumber under cool water. Pat dry.

3. **Arrange** carrots, tomatoes, and sugar snap peas on a serving plate. Be sure to leave room in the center for the bowl of dip.

4. Use a knife and a cutting board to cut the radishes and the cucumber. To cut the radishes, **slice** off the ends and discard them. Then add the radishes to the serving plate.

5. To cut the cucumber, **cut** off the ends and discard them. **Slice** the cucumber into ¼-inch-thick rounds. Cut enough to measure 1 cup. Arrange them on the serving plate.

6. **Remove** the dip from the refrigerator, uncover, and place in the center of the plate. Dip veggies and enjoy!

TRY THIS!
Use other favorite vegetables. Broccoli florets, cauliflower florets, red or yellow pepper slices, celery, or green beans are all super tasty with this dip.

To tone down the flavor of the dip, use only ½ teaspoon minced garlic.

serves 6 to 8

preparation time: 15 minutes
cooking time: 30 minutes

ingredients:

4 green tomatoes
2 eggs
½ cup milk
1 teaspoon salt
¼ teaspoon ground black pepper
½ teaspoon thyme
½ cup cornmeal
¼ cup bread crumbs
¼ cup canola oil
sour cream

equipment:

paper towels
serrated knife
cutting board
small mixing bowl
liquid measuring cup
2 forks
deep pie pan
measuring spoons
measuring cups—½ cup, ¼ cup
large frying pan
spatula
large serving plate

Fried Green Tomatoes

Enjoy this delicious treat in late summer or early fall, when unripe tomatoes are everywhere. Crispy on the outside and juicy on the inside, these fried green tomatoes taste like those you might find at fairs.

1. **Wash** tomatoes in cool water and pat dry.

2. Use a serrated knife and a cutting board to cut the tomatoes. First, **cut** out the green or brown circle on the top. Discard it. Then **cut** the rest of the tomato into slices ½-inch thick. Set aside.

3. **Crack** the eggs into a small mixing bowl. Add milk. Use a fork to **whisk** until well blended.

4. In a deep pie pan, combine salt, ground black pepper, thyme, cornmeal, and bread crumbs. Use a fork to **mix** well, being careful to keep the ingredients in the pan.

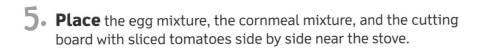

5. **Place** the egg mixture, the cornmeal mixture, and the cutting board with sliced tomatoes side by side near the stove.

6. **Pour** the canola oil into a large frying pan. Turn the burner under the frying pan on medium-high. Allow the frying pan to warm for 2 to 3 minutes. Meanwhile, **cover** a serving plate with 2 sheets of paper towels. Place the plate near the frying pan.

7. With your (clean) fingers, **dip** a tomato slice into the egg mixture until it is completely coated. Allow the drips to fall from the slice.

Turn the page for more Fried Green Tomatoes

Fried Green Tomatoes continued

8. Next, **dip** the egg-coated slice into the cornmeal mixture. Flip the slice over once to cover both sides.

9. Use the fork to **place** the slice in the hot frying pan. Watch out for splattering oil!

10. **Repeat** steps 7 to 9 until the frying pan is full of tomatoes. Be sure to leave a ½ inch between each tomato.

11. Cook the tomatoes for 5 to 7 minutes. Then use a spatula to **flip** the tomatoes over. Cook for another 5 to 7 minutes, until the tomatoes are light brown and crispy.

12. Use the spatula to **place** the fried tomatoes on the serving plate lined with paper towels. Repeat steps 7 to 11 with the rest of the slices. If needed, add additional oil to the frying pan for each new batch of tomatoes.

13. **Serve** the tomatoes warm with sour cream.

TRY THIS!

If green tomatoes aren't available, use large slices of **zucchini** or **eggplant** instead.

You can use **whole wheat** or **unbleached flour** instead of bread crumbs.

Vary the seasonings to taste. For spicier tomatoes, use **chili powder** or **Old Bay seasoning** instead of thyme.

SPECIAL INGREDIENTS

acorn squash: an acorn-shaped, dark green squash with ridges. Usually this type of squash is about the size of a softball. It can be found in the produce section of your grocery store.

broth or stock: the liquid part of a soup is called broth or stock. Look for it in the soup section of a grocery store. It comes in cans, cartons, and small jars.

celery salt: a celery-flavored seasoning found in the spice section of most grocery stores

cloves: a small, brown, spiky spice found in the spice section of most local grocery stores. Use whole cloves, not ground, for the refrigerator pickles recipe.

garlic, minced: chopped garlic in a jar. Jarred garlic is in the produce section of most grocery stores. If pre-minced garlic isn't available, buy fresh garlic. Peel away the papery skin, and ask your parents to chop the clove for you.

green tomatoes: tomatoes that have not yet ripened. Green tomatoes are usually not sold in grocery stores but are available from neighbors who garden or from farmers' markets at the end of the growing season.

half-and-half: a mixture of whole milk and cream. Cartons of half-and-half can be found in the dairy section of your grocery store.

kale: dark, curly, leafy greens found in the produce section of most grocery stores or food co-ops

mustard seeds: small yellow or tan seeds used to season foods. They can be found in the spice section of most grocery stores.

rice vinegar: a type of vinegar made from rice that has a slightly sweeter flavor than white vinegar. Rice vinegar can be found with the other vinegars and oils at your grocery store. It is also sold in most Asian grocery stores.

sweet potato: an orange-fleshed root vegetable that can be found in the produce section of most grocery stores

wild rice: a dark brown or black grain that grows on tall grasses in small lakes and streams. Wild rice can be found in the rice aisle of most grocery stores. If wild rice is too expensive, it's okay to use a wild rice blend instead.

Yukon gold potatoes: a variety of white potato with a buttery, yellow-colored flesh. Yukon golds are sold in the produce section of most grocery stores.

FURTHER READING AND WEBSITES

Choose My Plate
http://www.choosemyplate.gov/children-over-five.html
Download coloring pages, play an interactive computer game, and get lots of nutrition information at this U.S. Department of Agriculture website.

Farmers Markets
http://apps.ams.usda.gov/FarmersMarkets/
Visit this site to find a farmers' market near you!

Cleary, Brian P. *Food Is CATegorical* series. Minneapolis: Millbrook Press, 2011.
This seven-book illustrated series offers a fun introduction to the food groups and other important health information.

Katzen, Mollie. *Honest Pretzels: And 64 Other Recipes for Kids Ages 8 and Up.* Berkeley, CA: Tricycle Press, 2009.
This cookbook includes a whole bunch of vegetarian recipes.

Nissenberg, Sandra. *The Everything Kids' Cookbook: From Mac 'n Cheese to Double Chocolate Chip Cookies—90 Recipes to Have Some Finger-Lickin' Fun.* Avon: MA: Adams Media, 2008.
This cookbook is a great source for recipes kids love to make, including veggie side dishes.

INDEX

You're the Chef
Metric Conversions

VOLUME

⅛ teaspoon	0.62 milliliters
¼ teaspoon	1.2 milliliters
½ teaspoon	2.5 milliliters
¾ teaspoon	3.7 milliliters
1 teaspoon	5 milliliters
½ tablespoon	7.4 milliliters
1 tablespoon	15 milliliters
⅛ cup	30 milliliters
¼ cup	59 milliliters
⅓ cup	79 milliliters
½ cup	118 milliliters
⅔ cup	158 milliliters
¾ cup	177 milliliters
1 cup	237 milliliters
2 quarts (8 cups)	1,893 milliliters
3 fluid ounces	89 milliliters
12 fluid ounces	355 milliliters
24 fluid ounces	710 milliliters

MASS (weight)

1 ounce	28 grams
3.4 ounces	96 grams
3.5 ounces	99 grams
4 ounces	113 grams
7 ounces	198 grams
8 ounces	227 grams
12 ounces	340 grams
14.5 ounces	411 grams
15 ounces	425 grams
15.25 ounces	432 grams
16 ounces (1 pound)	454 grams
17 ounces	482 grams
21 ounces	595 grams

TEMPERATURE

Fahrenheit	Celsius
170°	77°
185°	85°
250°	121°
325°	163°
350°	177°
375°	191°
400°	204°
425°	218°
450°	232°

LENGTH

¼ inch	0.6 centimeters
½ inch	1.27 centimeters
1 inch	2.5 centimeters
2 inches	5 centimeters
3 inches	7.6 centimeters
5 inches	13 centimeters
8 inches	20 centimeters
9 x 11 inches	23 x 28 centimeters
9 x 13 inches	23 x 33 centimeters